TELLING MY FACE TO SMILE

JUDY SPENCER

Chicago Spectrum Press
Louisville, Kentucky

"The Parkinson's Awareness Association of Central Indiana, Inc., in conjunction with DuPont Pharma, is proud to sponsor Judy Spencer in the development and completion of this publication."

*–Parkinson's Awarness Association
of Central Indiana, Inc.*

Chicago Spectrum Press
4824 Brownsboro Center Arcade
Louisville, KY 40207
1-800-594-5190

Printed in the U.S.A.

10 9 8 7 6 5 4 3 2 1

ISBN: 1-58374-004-X

Cover art by Eve Spencer

In memory of my mother,
who suffered from undiagnosed Parkinson's Disease,
I dedicate this collection of poetry and prose,
to the Parkinson's Disease community,
to the doctors and nurses, the technicians
and therapists,
the researchers and activists,
the families and friends
the care-givers of all persuasion,
and all those folks who must face
living with Parkinson's Disease
every day.

ACKNOWLEDGMENTS

In the fall of 1992 I had the good fortune to spend an hour with famed doctor/author, Oliver Sacks, who encouraged me to read everything written by people with Parkinson's and then to ". . . perhaps write your own book—memoirs (and poems, I hope) written by people under pressure of illness are of immense value to others and to physicians. . ."

That conversation was a turning point in my life and I will forever be grateful to Dr. Sacks for giving me the idea and the permission I needed to even consider the possibility of publishing a book. He helped me find my passion for "Parky Poetry." And thank you Bob, for alerting me to Dr. Sacks' appearance on TV, which got the ball rolling.

I want to thank Sena and Mary and my writing group, especially Cynthia Castleman who edited a piece I wrote about my surgery. I am grateful to my friends Ellyn, Camie, Betty, Sherry, Alice and many more for making me realize that my poems did speak to readers.

Thanks go to Nancy and Marte, lifelong friends who cheered me on. I couldn't have finished this book without the meticulous help that my friends Marilyn, Eleanor, Hellene, and the Hoppers contributed. Thanks to "Dr. Lou," Karen, George, and Jo for their encouragement.

My siblings Joan, Dick, and Bob were advocates, readers, and fans from the beginning. Their enthusiasm for my work meant so much to me. Thanks to my nieces and nephews for their support, too, especially

Chris and her son Brad who helped with computer problems.

My children—Eve, Bill, Vicky, and Judy—have all encouraged me and helped make this happen. Eve, by designating me "writing mentor" to my grandson, inspired me to keep at it. (He's already published, at age seven.) Judy was the first to see my writing as a career and Bill valued my work as he explored the writing world. However, I never could have done it without Vicky, my computer guru and critic, who put up with my fears and occasional tears. She laughed with me, and rescued me time and time again and somehow managed to maintain her sanity.

And I want to thank my grandchildren—Ben, Gavin, and Kala—for their unending inspiration and little Liam for the thrill of new life and all the hope it brings.

I want to thank my doctor, Walter Olson, and Judy Olson for their kindness and concern and Prof. Barbara Oremland, PT, who gave me the opportunity to speak to the graduating physical therapists at the University of Louisville. Thanks also to Dr. Charles Oats who gave me my first speaking opportunity and Dr. John Cowan who enjoyed my humor so much. I am fortunate that I found Dr. Clifford Kuhn, the "Laugh Doctor," who has helped me realize the power of laughter.

I am particularly grateful to tennis pro Chuck Saacke who was the first to tell me about stereotactic pallidotomy surgery. And I am deeply grateful to my surgeon Dr. Reese Cosgrove who, through this procedure, gave me back my life. His confidence, skill, and caring made what for most people might be a frightening experience, the most exciting day of my life. I never could have continued my writing focus without that surgery. And thank you Bill and Joan for helping me find Dr. Cosgrove.

I would be remiss in my thanks if I did not include the wonderful people at St. Matthews Episcopal Church who nurtured me physically and spiritually and prayed for me so often. And when I was struggling to pull everything together for the publisher, the visiting Rev. James Warnke blessed my work and helped me find the spiritual energy to go on.

Finally, I want to thank Bonnie Gordon from DuPont and Julie Sanderson, John Deck, and PAICI for sponsoring my book and helping me get a grant from the DuPont Company, which has generously funded the publication of this book.

CONTENTS

WRITING TO CELEBRATE

WRITING TO COMPREHEND

HELLO

I was not
much past thirty-nine.
It was a demanding time,
aging parents,
ailing marriage,
rebellious teens,
swim teams,
vans and braces,
pimply faces.

I figured I could manage.
I was at my prime,
but I wasn't feeling so fine.
First it was my hands
that wouldn't work
then I seemed to walk with a jerk.

"Parkinsons Disease,"
the doctor said.
"It's a movement disorder.
It's chronic.
It's progressive.
It's incurable. It's bad!"

Parky and I have been
together for a couple of decades now.
He has made a writer of me.
He has made a fighter of me.
I have learned that sometimes it's best
to accommodate his inconsistencies,
to laugh and play with his eccentricities.
He has taught me the very real power of prayer
and how many good people there are out there.
It has been a surprise for me to realize
how much Parky has enriched this life of mine.
I hope my poems will lighten your life with Parky. . .
just a little bit.

Judy

June, 1999

I HAVE PARKINSON'S DISEASE

And I want
you to know it.
Because often,
you'll see,
I show it.

When I walk
like a drunk
and I talk
like a drunk,
it's just me trying
to move
with that monster
PD.

1995

L-DOPA AND ME

A miracle drug
of the sixties,
it makes my body
work, it makes my body j—
e—
r—
k—

without it, I
freeze or I shake,
too much and I
wobble. I c
R
a
S
h and I stumble.

Daily I search for that dose where I'm ON
when it works with no jerks.

1994

A RIDDLE

Sometimes L-dopa
makes a
dopa
of
me.

1994

DENIAL

My children, and friends
say, "Hey, you look great!"
as I stumble and shake.
Is it my fears or theirs
they seek to alleviate?

1994

ALONE

I walk alone
for to tell you
the truth,
I really want to,
I really need to,
I really have to.

1995

MOTHER MAY I

Take giant steps,
jump for joy,
sing out,
hop about,
shout.

1995

IN THE MORNING

I am lost
in space,
in my very own
place. I must
load up on
sinemet,
then I can
walk and
talk.

1994

MY WALK

The time is
right, the
On is in.
My ritual walk
must begin.

All together
hopefully, please,
I'd like to just
walk and look at
the trees.

Arms swinging,
eyes blinking,
I'm a walker.
I'm just being.

Swing left with
right, right with
left. Ah, there's
a robin, it's
in flight.

Left, right, left,
Heel toe, heel toe,
there's a neighbor
driving by. Smile,
face, and wave
"hello."

Turn the corner,
face the wind.
Blink, eye lids,
blink. Blink left,
blink right. . .

Swing left, swing
right. Slow down,
catch up.
Get it right.
Now get it
right.

Blooming dogwoods
up ahead, on the right.
such a sight, on
the RIGHT . . .
LEFT . . . right . . .

On the right
. . . heel,
toe, on . . .

swing left . . .RIGHT,
Nothing . . . left . . .

Try, "HEEL, toe
heel . . .
toe,". . . It's off,
. . . my ON
is OFF, my swing
has swung.

1994

CARDS

I like to
play bridge.
But Parky always
wants to come.

I can't shuffle.
I shouldn't deal.
My partner and I are
vulnerable, before
we ever start.

It would be a
grand slam if
I could finesse
this pest
and just play
Bridge.

1994

NOCTURNAL HALLUCINATIONS

There's an army in
my mattress. It keeps
marching through
my head.

Sheets and blankets
rise and fall as the
soldiers pass
below.

Monsters, fools,
and kitty cats
gather at my bed.
They come to stalk
that army, hiding
in my head.

date?

IT'S MY OWN FAULT

And, the epicenter is
under my bed, under
my house . . . in
my head?

Every night,
vibrations
make my bedroom
shake.

I lie there
frozen,
waiting for
the quake.

1994

WRITING TO TELL

WHEN I'M OFF

I can't move me.
But if a gentle giant
would, he could
move me.
Like a child's
small hand
can move
his toy train
should its electricity
be off complicity.

1998

MARIONETTE

When I'm off,
like a marionette,
I need
someone to
pull my strings,
make my arms
move like wings,
lift my knees
so I can dance in the
breeze,
make all of me
move with the cadence
of life's repeats

1998

JUMPING ROPE

Left. . . Left. He
left his wife and
forty eight kids, at
home in the kitchen
in starving condition
without any gingerbread . . .

Left. . . Left. I Left
my purse and forty-eight pills at home
in the kitchen
and now my condition
reveals my affliction,
there's no dopamine. . . left. . .
Left. . . Left.

1994

THE GREATEST THREAT

Seeing, touching,
talking, walking,
and the greatest
of these is . . .

talking.
Lungs, larynx,
tongue, I have
my talking
team.

I have them all.
But, Parky lies
in wait to mess
with any call.
Now

talking is
another verb
at risk in my
shrinking ways
of linking.

1995

RUSHING IN SLOW MOTION

Imagine . . .
washing your
hair,
folding
sheets,
chopping celery,
Slowly.

Imagine . . .
planting
wild flowers,
tying a toddler's
shoe laces,
opening a carton of
ice cream, ever so
Slowly.

Imagine . . .
pulling your
pants up,
turning pages in
the hymnal,
expressing joy, very,
Very Slowly.

Imagine one hour of
your life in
S-L-O-W M-O-T-I-O-N

1995

MAYBE

Headache, heartache,
backache,
depression, constipation,
sexual frustration,
low energy, no energy,
dry skin, dry eyes,
dry mouth, toothache,
tummyache . . . .

Blame it all on
Parky.
Maybe I shouldn't.
Maybe I
should.

1995

ENERGY

I'm So Bossy
I tell my face to smile,
I tell my feet to walk,
I even tell my mouth to talk.

I'm so busy bossing me,
I use up all my energy
telling every part, you see
when to move,
and how to be.

1998

On the Subject of Staying Awake
I'm hopin'
I can keep my
eyes open.

1998

THE FREEZE

Feet planted,
body hurling forward,
some law of physics
must be broken.

1996

FAST FORWARD

Coming out of a freeze
I'm moving fast,
if you please.
I may look like a clown
but I could run you down.
The danger is there.
We both must take care.
Watch out when I'm moving in
fast forward!

1999

A PARKY SHINER

Crossing the
asphalt drive,
my feet got
stuck, I took a
dive.

Bruised and
scared,
it made
me cry.
I was lucky,
my friend
was nearby.

1995

PEOPLE WATCHING

I always noticed clothes,
faces, attitudes,
places.

Now I watch
how people walk
and talk . . .
  with ease.

1995

IN MY OTHER LIFE

I was a facilitator
and I did not
know it.
I only found out
when I no longer
could and no
one else would.

1995

TRYING

When every step is a chore,
and you have three or four more
to navigate and you hear
someone say, "I don't think
you are trying today."
You realize they still don't
understand this disease
and how sometimes you can
and sometimes you can't
do what you did
yesterday,
or five minutes ago.

1999

RSVP

Parties are made of
voices and faces,
standing in
places,
drinks to
spill and food
to finger,
dancing feet,
folks to
meet,
colors
and clothes
flowers and
smells . . .
        RSVP
        Ms. Me regrets

A PARTY

for me, is
just two
or three.
Any more
and I run for
the door,

if I can.

1997

LET'S MONITOR

Monitor your "ons,"
Monitor your "offs,"
Every fifteen minutes.
Let's monitor.
Monitor your meds,
Sinemet the "King."
Does he help you work?
Or does he make you jerk?
The agonists,
Do they make you better?
And what about
The weather?
Monitor, yes, monitor!

Monitor your food.
What's your mood?
Did you sleep well?
Can you pee well?
Did you go?
Did you freeze?
Did you sneeze?
Monitor, every fifteen minutes,
Let's monitor.

How's your walk?
Can you talk?
Can you swoller?
Can you holler?
If you choke
You could croak.
But, don't forget,
First, make a note!
Monitor, yes, monitor.
Every fifteen minutes,
Let's Monitor!

1998

WHEN THE DOCTOR DOESN'T CALL

You rehearse all day
what you need to say.
You write it down
and carry it around.
You stay off the phone
you do not leave,
you are afraid
to bathe or shower.

I wonder if the doctor
knows the power
of his missing call?

1998

WHY I LOST THIRTY POUNDS

Dinner Alone
Lurch and Pray
from couch to TV
to kitchen counter.
Now edge along, edge along
to the refrigerator.
Reach for a treat
something easy to
eat. Dine right
there, no need for a chair.
Now edge back,
edge back,
lurch and pray,
lurch and pray,
back to the couch,
it's such a long way.
But, three cheers,
I've made it today.

Lunch
Food can't nurture much
when you have
wiggles with lunch.

1996

WHEN YOU LOOSE YOUR GAIT

Concentrate
Step out and count
one and two and three and four,
heel and toe, heel, and toe.
Go slow, go slow.
Instruct your knee to lift up high.
Now tell your foot to pass on by.
Heel and toe, heel and toe,
count as you go
Go slow, go slow.
Concentrate
Don't even talk,
Work on your walk.

Remember, when you loose
your gait, concentrate!

1996

OPERATE

When you're over fifty-five,
and living in a body
only half-alive,
a body that can seldom
cooperate.
What do you do?
Operate!

When the medicine
doesn't work,
you're either frozen
or you jerk.
When you are declared
"Queen of Fluctuation," and
there is little celebration,
What do you do?
Operate!

Don't wait
till it's
too late.
Operate.

1996

WRITING TO CELEBRATE

I KNEW I COULD

I knew I could.
I knew I would,
get well again.
Thank God, I am
well again.
To walk again,
to talk again.
I knew I could.
I knew I would
be me again
and do again,
do well
again.
Thank God
again.
Amen,
Amen again.

1996

*This poem is a Thanksgiving prayer written after I underwent successful surgery for advanced Parkinson's Disease. It is written in the tradition of *The Little Engine That Could.*

THIS IS ONLY TEMPORARY

I was wiggly, I was weepy, I was weak.
but I always knew, "This is only temporary."
I could barely put my clothes on.
I could barely take them off.
I needed help getting in the car,
fastening the seat belt,
unfastening the seat belt,
I needed help paying bills,
writing notes.

And there were so many helpers.
So many to thank, so many to remind,
"This is only temporary."
Thank you God for all those friends
who helped, even though they did not
and could not believe,
this was only
temporary.

1996

OPTIONS

L-dopa, carbidopa,
sinmet, sinemet C.R.
Pallidotomys, implants,
the agonists, combination therapy,
the new synthetic agents . . .
physical therapy, psyco-therapy, bio-feedback,
food therapy, water aerobics,
grief therapy, yoga, ti chi and
tee hee, laughter therapy.

There is always something
more to try,
which might help us
live better till we die.

1999

AFTER BIO-FEEDBACK

I've tossed my cane,
I can drive,
even in the rain.
I'm flossing, I'm reading,
I'm busy, I'm steaming.
No problems too large,
'Cause I'm in charge.
Hooray for the computer!
Hooray for the doctor!
Let's celebrate!
Let's celebrate!

1997

MY FAVORITE EXERCISE

I went to the Laugh Doctor
and he told me to laugh.
It's good for your body.
It's good for your head,
The very happy Laugh
Doctor said.
So I laughed and I laughed.
I laughed when life was funny.
I laughed when it was not.
I laughed when I
should, and I laughed when
I shouldn't.
I laughed till I cried.
I wore myself out.
I might die laughing
if I don't watch out.
My children fussed.
My neighbors wondered.
I think I actually scared my
little granddaughter.
But my body cheered.
My blood pressure jumped.
A healthier, happier me
was the very happy result.

1999

LAUGHING ALL THE WAY

LAUGHING ALL THE WAY

It was at a health center, at one of the local malls that I first heard Dr. Clifford Kuhn, the Laugh Doctor, talk about the biology of laughter. After his hilarious presentation, he gave an assignment: "Laugh half an hour a day."

He promised that would make us happier and healthier. A few months later, on a trip to Disney World, I had an opportunity to experience first hand the therapeutic power of laughter.

I had no trouble accumulating half an hour of laughing a day. In fact I could not stop laughing. I laughed all the way from the Magic Kingdom, through MGM and on to Epcot. The day after my return I saw my neurologist. He was so amazed at my energy level and my neurological dexterity that he insisted I tell this story.

It all began when my daughter Vicky suggested that we take her foster child Kala and my six year old grandson, Ben, to Disney World. Since I have Parkinson's Disease, my energy is often in short supply. Though I was able to retire my wheelchair after successful brain surgery in 1996, I still have the disease and I need to take medicine every two hours. If I don't get my pills just right I might have trouble walking or talking, and start wiggling. So you can imagine my hesitation when Vicky proposed this adventure.

Kala was a month shy of six when she cartwheeled into our lives. All she needed to do was come through my front door and I felt my energy level take a nose dive. And Ben had been performing intellectual cartwheels ever since he was a toddler. His nonstop commentary drained my mental energy. My immediate answer to Vicky's idea was, "I'd be brain dead by the end of the first day."

But, Vicky had it all figured out. "We'll get a hotel right next to Epcot. You can come back at noon and take a nap and I can take over with the kids."

She had studied the handicapped brochure and was convinced that with the help of my old wheelchair I could do it. She proposed a five day trip in October when it would not be terribly hot or crowded. It was a stretch for me, but when I was able to get health postponement insurance, I signed on. Had I any idea how therapeutic an adventure it would turn out to be I would not have hesitated.

We arrived in Florida aboard Delta Express, in a major downpour. A friend had volunteered to buy groceries and meet us at the airport. I was delighted with her very thoughtful offer. But it took some very clever arranging to pack my wheelchair, all our bags and the four of us into her little car without crushing the six bags of groceries. When we got to our hotel we looked like the little circus car with all the clowns tumbling out of it. Fortunately, the weather had cleared.

Kala, "Miss Bossy Britches," tried to take over the minute we got to our expensive little suite. She wanted to play house, Ben wanted to play dinosaurs (at age four, Benjamin had declared himself a paleontologist.)

They compromised. They played house and the babies were dinosaurs.

I thought we were off to a good start. I had survived the "getting there" stresses and was enjoying the juxtaposition that our two hyperactive charges took on almost every turn of events. But I think that was the last compromise. Every move we made from that point on was negotiated. The wheelchair inspired endless argument—"I get to push Grandma!"—"No, I get to push Grandma"—and led to some of my scariest rides at Disney.

Our first full day, we hauled my wheelchair on and off boats, up and down countless ramps, over numerous curbs, on and off the monorail, and in and out of several buses as we explored the Magic Kingdom. That evening, when we left the hotel for our big dinner date with Chef Mickey, a "must do," the wheelchair balked at being folded and shoved around anymore. In our hurry at the monorail station, we parked it in a fenced-in corral area and left.

After a little eating (Kala spilled her entire plate on the way back from the buffet line), much singing, dancing, hugging, and kissing with all of Mickey's buddies, especially Chip and Dale, we left the restaurant in festive spirits.

We were off to recover my wheelchair and then on to the Electric Parade. We hopped back on the monorail and quickly arrived at the station where we remembered leaving the wheelchair. But, guess what? No wheelchair! I thought I spotted it in a corral on the other side of the tracks. In an emergency measure, a Disney employee stopped the monorail, opened up the doors on both sides to form a bridge over the tracks, and ushered our little group through and over to the other side..

After two more such maneuvers and still no wheelchair, Ben scratched his head thoughtfully and said. "We went the wrong way, Grandma!" (Every group needs at least one person with a sense of direction.)

Back we went and there it was, cowering in wounded repose in the corral where we had left it... on the other side of the tracks. One more special passage was arranged and we were reunited. With help from yet another nice Disney staffer we pushed, shoved, and banged the wheelchair into action one last time before retiring it to our suite for the duration of our stay.

I think it was on the third "special passage" through the monorail that Grandma started losing it. The image of us running through those cars, sometimes dragging the kids, sometimes charging, four abreast, was more than I could handle. I started laughing. I mean out of control nonstop laughing. It was the beginning of what was to become a pattern with me.

Whenever things started falling apart, and you can count on that happening when you travel with two six year olds, I would see something funny in the situation that no one else seemed to see. Within seconds I would be almost prone with laughter. You know, the often soundless, fall-down-on-the- ground, dying-of-laughter kind of laughing. Vicky, a great laugher herself, did not find these episodes funny. The kids did not know what to make of them and neither did I.

"Mom, what in the world got into you? What's with all this laughing?" Vicky asked. It was after ten and we were camped out on the balcony waiting for our roommates to go to sleep.

"I can't explain it," I confessed "but it's better than growling or crying. I didn't even take a nap. Look at what time it is—I am still walking and talking. I haven't lost my gait all day so I haven't needed my cane. All things considered, I should be almost comatose."

"I knew you could do it," my daughter proclaimed. We discussed the day's adventures and made plans for the next day. The last thing Vicky said before we tiptoed back in was, "But, please Mom, no more laughing fits."

After that first day, I managed to arrive at whatever transportation we needed to get to our chosen destination—The Magic Kingdom, Epcot, or MGM, Then once we got there, we would rent a wheelchair (there was just too much walking for a "Parky"). This made us eligible for handicapped entry into all the rides which delighted Miss Bossy Britches. Always marching ahead of us, she started taking it upon herself to break into the crowds with a very important sounding, "Excuse me, EXCUSE ME! My grandmother (this was one of the times when I was lavished with that full title) has a DISEASE! Excuse me!" Of course, my "pushers" were rewarded for their altruistic efforts by not having to wait in lines.

One evening we were just turning onto the main pathway through Epcot, a child on either side of the wheelchair, Vicky pushing, when all of a sudden, as if choreographed by some invisible director, Ben and Kala broke into a wild jig, hopping and jumping about like tree frogs celebrating in the rain.. When I tried to get an explanation for this outburst, Ben informed me that they had been sprayed with Goofy Spray, and there was nothing they could do about it.

We were all enjoying the fun until Kala started turning cartwheels. My efforts at control with "Goofy Off Spray" did not bring things to a halt. Vicky turned into a storm cloud and I started laughing. It wasn't until we had been back home in Louisville for a few weeks when Ben confided in me that he and Kala had been sprayed with Goofy Spray because they are members of a secret "Goofy Club."

By the end of the second day, not only had we managed to break my wheelchair, but my cane was lost as well, and neither of those seemingly disastrous turn of events had slowed us down. I was walking and talking like a normal person. The only shaking I was doing was associated with my laughing Something more than magical was happening to me at this magical place. I was getting very little rest staying up reading till all hours, participating in everything. Where was all this energy coming from?

That evening we had supper in our suite. The kids were eating in front of the TV and not paying much attention to their meal. Vicky was getting impatient. "If you don't settle down something is going to hap. . ." when without warning, as if anxious to prove Vicky's point, Ben suddenly somersaulted off the couch into the coffee table. His plate and all the food on it flew up in the air before crashing to the floor in pieces.

It was the timing that got to me. I knew better than to look at Vicky. But she looked at me and could see that I was struggling to stay serious. Before the incident was over, Ben and I both landed in "Time Out."

The balcony review was a bit heated that night. "You are a bigger problem than the kids!" Vicky barked. I was beginning to feel very guilty, but what could I do?

The Laught Doctor did not say anything about how to stop laughing. We decided that the next evening Vicky would indulge in some sanity time away from the kids and their laughing grandma.

After days of anticipating the dinosaur show, we finally found the giants hiding out at The Universe of Energy in Epcot. Of course Ben was thrilled. "These are the coolest dinosaurs! This place is loaded with technology!" he shrieked. I think it was then that I began to realize that I had found my own Universe of energy in laughter.

Climbing into a diver's suit at the aquarium and coming face to face with a manatee and a giant eel gained high adventure status also. But it was Splash Mountain that remained the children's favorite ride from the very first day on. They made it quite clear that it was the terror Grandma experienced on this five story wet vertical plunge that took the ride to it's "Best!" status. It had been their turn to double-up laughing. But I, for one, was just happy to climb off the little boat with my neck and back apparently still aligned.

The last day presented a lot of stress. We needed to check out by eleven, but our flight did not leave until four o'clock and there were some things we still wanted to do at Epcot. So we managed to pack and check out by nine thirty.

We had an exciting morning at Planet Earth and then we stopped for lunch. Vicky parked us at a table and went off to get the food. Ben started expounding on the Black Hole theory, and Kala wanted to talk about where Mickey, Chip, and Dale were. All of a sudden tempers flared and my grandchildren were in a major boxing match. I stopped the fight just in time for Vicky's return with the food.

Feeling very proud of myself for my masterful handling of the situation, I was unprepared when Vicky decided to blow up because I hadn't gotten napkins and straws while she got the food. We were all ready to attack each other, when a large Coke went over right into Vicky's plate We were in "melt down." It occurred to me that any one watching would have been either horrified or laughing as hard as I wanted to. In a desperate effort to contain myself, I fantasized that we were already on the plane and everyone was behaving, even Grandma.

Just an hour later, we were playing our own, Disney Trivia game on the way to the airport when the cab driver told us we were the jolliest group he had ever transported. "You should have seen us an hour ago." I tried to explain to the driver, but I found myself caught up in yet one more laughing attack, unable to complete my story.

Once we got to the Delta gate, Vicky took a picture of me with my two ever-willing instruments of hilarity sporting their Mickey and Minnie mouse hats. Then with one shot left in our cameras, we posed Vicky, in a mouse hat. We took lots of good pictures on our trip, but that wasn't one of them. I cut Vicky's head off. I was very upset at first, but when Vicky found this turn of events hilarious, I readily joined in.

So where did all that energy come from? "The laughing energized you!" my neurologist concluded.

I'm still laughing and I heartily recommend the Laugh Doctor's assignment. Laugh all the way, wherever you are.

Help!

Wiggles with Lunch.

A Parky doing "The Freeze."

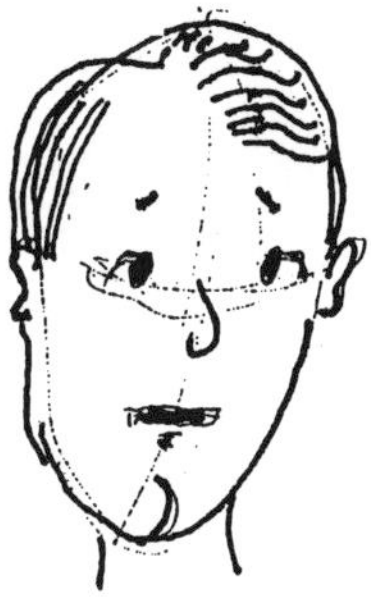

A Parky doing "The Smile."

The Queen of Fluctuation